W9-BFX-417

NEW YORK JETS

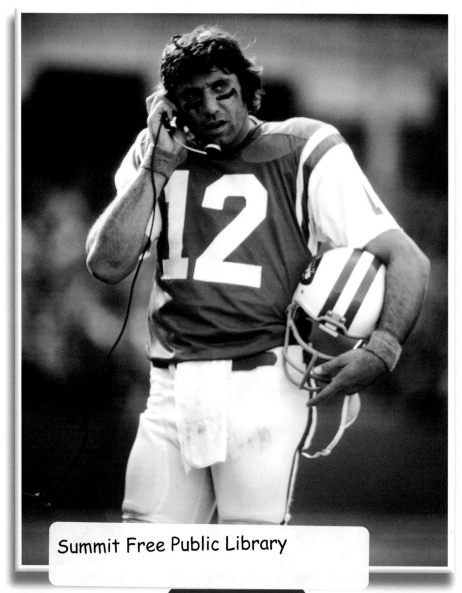

by Tom Robinson

Published by ABDO Publishing Company, 8000 West 78th Street, Edina, Minnesota 55439. Copyright © 2011 by Abdo Consulting Group, Inc. International copyrights reserved in all countries. No part of this book may be reproduced in any form without written permission from the publisher. SportsZone™ is a trademark and logo of ABDO Publishing Company.

Printed in the United States of America,
North Mankato, Minnesota
062010
122011

Editor: Matt Tustison
Copy Editor: Nicholas Cafarelli
Interior Design and Production: Kazuko Collins
Cover Design: Christa Schneider

Photo Credits: Evan Pinkus/AP Images, cover; NFL Photos/AP Images, title page, 4, 10, 42 (top); AP Images, 7, 9, 15, 16, 18, 21, 24, 42 (bottom), 43 (top); File/AP Images, 12, 42 (middle); Scott Halleran/Getty Images, 22, 43 (middle); Bill Kostroun/AP Images, 26, 33, 34, 43 (bottom), 47; John Greilick/AP Images, 28; John Greilich/AP Images, 31; David Zalubowski/AP Images, 36; Kathy Willens, File/AP Images, 39; Denis Poroy/AP Images, 41; Kevin Rivoli/AP Images, 44

Library of Congress Cataloging-in-Publication Data
Robinson, Tom.
  New York Jets / Tom Robinson.
     p. cm. — (Inside the NFL)
  Includes index.
  ISBN 978-1-61714-022-8
  1. New York Jets (Football team)—History—Juvenile literature. I. Title.
  GV956.N37R63 2010
  796.332'64097471—dc22
                                    2010017370

TABLE OF CONTENTS

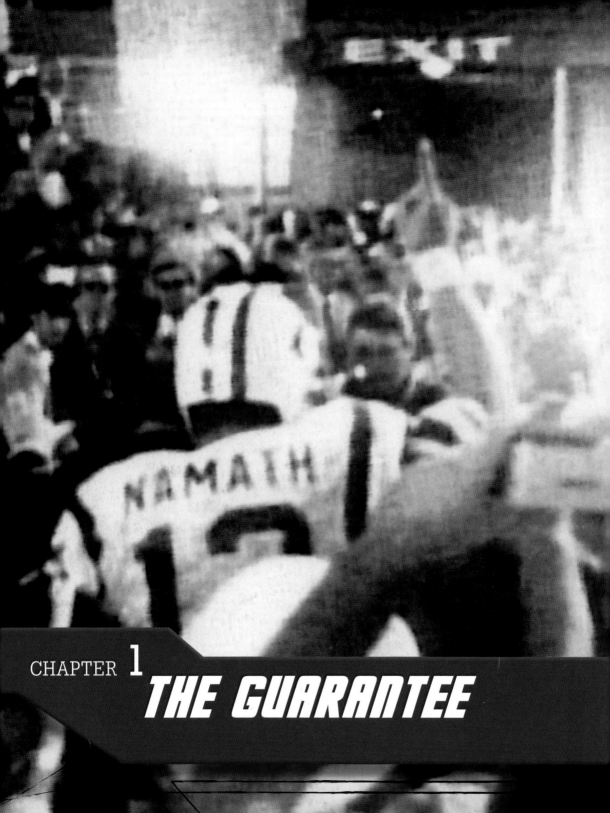

CHAPTER 1
THE GUARANTEE

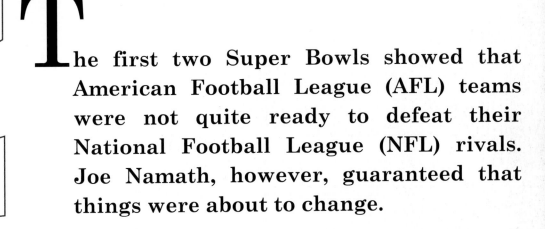

The first two Super Bowls showed that American Football League (AFL) teams were not quite ready to defeat their National Football League (NFL) rivals. Joe Namath, however, guaranteed that things were about to change.

Namath's New York Jets had won the AFL championship in 1968. They were set to play the NFL-champion Baltimore Colts in Super Bowl III on January 12, 1969, in Miami, Florida. In the two weeks leading up to the big game, the constant talk was about how the Colts were simply too strong for the Jets. Namath went to the Miami Touchdown Club to receive an award the Thursday night before Super Bowl Sunday. As Namath

FEELING SUPERIOR

The Green Bay Packers had helped create the impression that the National Football League was much stronger than the American Football League. The Vince Lombardi-coached Packers had handled the AFL champions in the first two Super Bowls. They beat the Kansas City Chiefs 35–10 and the Oakland Raiders 33–14.

JETS QUARTERBACK JOE NAMATH SIGNALS THAT HIS TEAM IS NUMBER ONE AFTER IT DEFEATED THE HEAVILY FAVORED COLTS 16–7 IN SUPER BOWL III.

COMPARING THE LEAGUES

The NFL began in 1920 as the American Professional Football Association. Its name was changed to the National Football League in 1922. The league had 16 teams before its merger with the American Football League in 1970.

The AFL debuted in 1960. It grew from eight teams that year to 10 in its final season.

In the merger to form one league in 1970, three teams had to join with the former AFL teams to form the new American Football Conference (AFC). The Baltimore Colts, Cleveland Browns, and Pittsburgh Steelers made the switch. The remaining 13 teams became known as the National Football Conference (NFC).

The league kept the National Football League as its name. The AFC and NFC have been part of the NFL ever since. Their champions meet each year in the Super Bowl.

headed for the microphone, a fan heckled him about how much stronger the Colts were. The remarks drew laughter from the audience.

The 25-year-old quarterback told the crowd he was tired of hearing about it. He did not stop there. "We're gonna win the game," Namath said. "I guarantee it."

After that, there was little else to talk about besides Namath's bold prediction until the Super Bowl was played.

There were reasons the Colts were favored by about 19 points. First, Baltimore was from the NFL. That league had been around much longer than the AFL. It had also easily produced the first two Super Bowl winners.

The Colts also had a record of 13–1 in the tougher league.

JETS QUARTERBACK JOE NAMATH, *LEFT*, WARMS UP AT PRACTICE IN FORT LAUDERDALE, FLORIDA, WITH TIGHT END PETE LAMMONS TWO DAYS BEFORE SUPER BOWL III.

The Jets went 11–3 in the AFL. In the NFL Championship Game, Baltimore hammered the Cleveland Browns 34–0. The NFL's top-ranked defense figured to be too strong for the offense run by Namath.

Namath was considered flashy. His nicknames included "Broadway Joe." The Jets beat the Colts without much flash from Namath, however. They used solid, basic football to pull off one of the greatest upsets in pro football history.

The defense held Baltimore scoreless in the first half. Namath passed well. The running of Matt Snell was just as important, though. When it came time to protect a lead in the fourth quarter, Namath did not throw a pass. The Jets ran time off the clock to finish the 16–7 victory. Namath finished 17-for-28 passing for 206 yards. George Sauer had eight catches for 133 yards. Snell carried 30 times for 121 more yards and a touchdown. Namath was given credit for changing many plays at the line of scrimmage. This countered Baltimore's aggressive defense.

On the biggest day of his career and in the Jets' history, Namath was selected as Most Valuable Player (MVP) of the Super Bowl. The Super Bowl came about because the NFL and AFL had agreed in 1966 that they would merge into one larger league. There was uncertainty, though, whether the combined league would create even competition. And there were concerns about whether the Super Bowl would develop the popularity worthy of a championship game. Namath's guarantee gave more people a reason to watch Super Bowl III. The Jets' win gave more people a reason to watch professional football in the future.

DON MAYNARD

The AFL came around just in time for Don Maynard. The former Texas Western College star had lasted just one season in the NFL after being drafted by the New York Giants. The wide receiver then spent the 1959 season in the Canadian Football League. He became an original member of the New York Titans in 1960. The Titans would later change their name to the Jets. Maynard succeeded right away in the AFL. He later clicked with quarterback Joe Namath. Both would be inducted into the Pro Football Hall of Fame.

JETS QUARTERBACK JOE NAMATH HANDS OFF TO FULLBACK MATT SNELL
IN SUPER BOWL III. SNELL RAN FOR 121 YARDS IN THE GAME.

By the time the 1970 season started, a little more than a year and half a later, the AFL was gone. It had become part of the NFL. With help from Namath and the Jets, the new NFL was on its way to becoming the most popular pro sports league in the United States.

One of the most famous victories in professional football history was produced by a team that was created less than a decade earlier.

CHAPTER 2

TAKING OFF

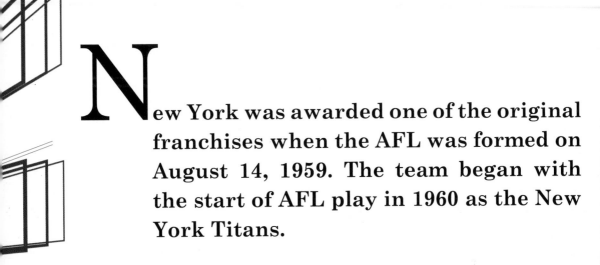

New York was awarded one of the original franchises when the AFL was formed on August 14, 1959. The team began with the start of AFL play in 1960 as the New York Titans.

By 1962, the Titans were losing on the field and struggling in attendance. After two 7–7 seasons in a row, they went just 5–9 in 1962. Before their third season was over, the Titans were in danger of extinction. Owner Harry Wismer was unable to pay his team and employees. The AFL took over the costs of running the bankrupt operation from November 8 to the end of the 1962 season.

THE FIRST YEAR

The New York Titans defeated the Buffalo Bills 27–3 in their first game on September 11, 1960. The Titans finished their first season 7–7. Don Maynard caught 72 passes to lead the team. Maynard and Art Powell formed the first professional wide receiver combination to each catch passes for 1,000 or more yards on the same team in the same season.

WIDE RECEIVER DON MAYNARD WAS A STANDOUT PLAYER FOR THE NEW YORK TITANS/JETS FRANCHISE IN ITS BEGINNING YEARS.

JETS COACH/GENERAL MANAGER WEEB EWBANK, *LEFT*, AND OWNER
SONNY WERBLIN ARE ALL SMILES AS QUARTERBACK JOE NAMATH SIGNS
WITH THE TEAM ON JANUARY 2, 1965.

The team's name, the Titans, was gone before the 1963 season. But the team remained. David A. "Sonny" Werblin led a five-man group that purchased the team for $1 million on March 28, 1963.

On April 15, the new owners named Weeb Ewbank as their coach and general manager. Ewbank had formerly been the Baltimore Colts' coach. The new owners also changed the team's name from Titans to Jets. The team was planning to eventually move to Shea Stadium. It was located between New York's two biggest airports, making the name "Jets" appropriate.

The results on the field changed little, however. The 1962 Titans were 5–9. The team went 5–8–1 in each of the next three seasons. Positive changes were starting to occur, though.

The Jets whipped the Denver Broncos 30–6 in their debut at Shea on September 12, 1964. The talent level of the Jets' players was on the rise. After each of the first two seasons under new ownership, the Jets drafted and signed the player who would go on to be the AFL Rookie of the Year the next season. In the days before the AFL's merger into the NFL, the leagues drafted players separately. Teams from those leagues would then often battle to get a player signed.

The Jets chose Matt Snell with their first pick in the 1964 AFL Draft. The fullback from Ohio State was also selected

JOE NAMATH

Joe Namath brought excitement to professional football. Namath was nicknamed "Broadway Joe" for the attention he received while enjoying the New York City nightlife. On the field, Namath was known most for two things. The first was the Super Bowl III upset victory that he guaranteed and delivered. The second was his battle with knee injuries.

Namath was the AFL Rookie of the Year in 1965. He led the Jets to their first Eastern Division and AFL championships in 1968. He followed them up with the 16–7 Super Bowl win over the Baltimore Colts in January of 1969. He was the AFL Player of the Year in the championship season, which he capped as MVP of the Super Bowl.

Namath threw for 27,663 yards and 173 touchdowns in 12 seasons with the Jets and a final season with the Los Angeles Rams in 1977.

by New York's NFL team, the Giants. His signing marked the first time the Titans/Jets franchise was able to keep the first player it selected. Snell rushed for 948 yards and caught 56 passes on the way to his Rookie of the Year award in 1964.

The Jets were not finished. On January 2, 1965, New York signed quarterback Joe Namath. This happened one day after Namath's unbeaten University of Alabama team had fallen

21–17 to the University of Texas in the Orange Bowl. The contract was reportedly worth $427,000. It was a pro football record at the time.

Namath had played in pain during his senior year at Alabama. He had knee surgery in New York within a month of signing with the Jets.

After making his pro debut starting the Jets' second game, Namath completed less than half his passes that rookie season. However, he did throw for 2,220 yards and 18 touchdowns.

The Jets started showing improvement with Namath running the offense. The 1966 team started out 4–0–1, only to slip to a 6–6–2 final record. A loss in the 1967 opener was followed by a six-game unbeaten streak to propel the Jets to 5–1–1. By Thanksgiving, the team

THE *HEIDI* GAME

The Jets lost just once in their final 11 games during the 1968 season. That loss came against the Oakland Raiders in one of pro football's most famous games. The game became famous because NBC cut off the television broadcast with 50 seconds left. The Jets had kicked a field goal to take a 32–29 lead just 15 seconds earlier. With the outcome still undecided, NBC kept to its advertised schedule. It aired the children's movie Heidi at 7:00 p.m. The broadcast ended, but the Raiders did not stop. They scored twice in the last 42 seconds for a 43–32 victory.

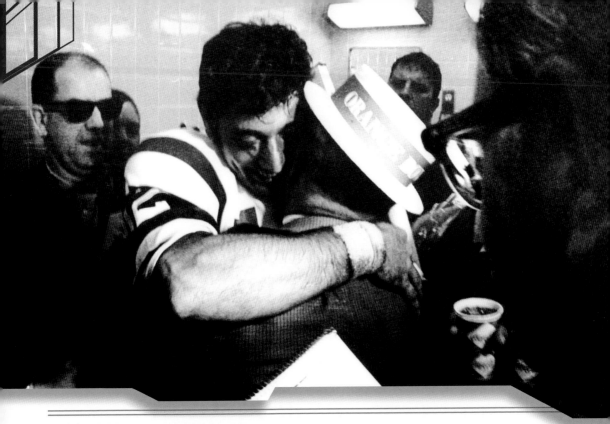

JOE NAMATH GIVES HIS FATHER, JOHN, A HUG AFTER THE JETS STUNNED THE COLTS 16–7 IN SUPER BOWL III IN JANUARY 1969.

had clinched its first winning season.

When Namath threw for 343 yards in a season-ending 42–31 victory over the San Diego Chargers, the Jets finished 8–5–1. Namath became the first professional quarterback to pass for more than 4,000 yards in a season, with 4,007.

The Jets began their 1968 season 3–2. They recovered to finish 11–3. It was good enough for first place in the Eastern Division and a spot in the AFL Championship Game. After a 27–23 title game victory over the Oakland Raiders, the Jets went on to record their historic win over the Baltimore Colts in Super Bowl III.

CHAPTER **3**

JOINING THE NFL

The NFL and AFL played one more season as separate leagues after the Jets won Super Bowl III. The 1969 Jets went 10–4 to repeat as Eastern Division champions. However, they lost 13–6 to the Kansas City Chiefs in the AFL semifinals. When the 1969 season was over, the leagues joined together in 1970.

All the old AFL teams stayed together in the American Football Conference (AFC). The Jets were placed in the East, one of three divisions in the AFC. The Jets, Boston Patriots, Buffalo Bills, and Miami Dolphins stayed together. They were joined by the Baltimore Colts, who moved over from the old NFL. The division rivals would face each other twice every season.

MONDAY NIGHT FOOTBALL DEBUT

The Jets opened the 1970 season by playing the Cleveland Browns, a new member of the AFC, in the debut of ABC television's Monday Night Football. The host Browns won 31–21.

QUARTERBACK JOE NAMATH LED THE JETS AS THEY JOINED THE NFL IN 1970. THEY WOULD NOT MATCH THE SUCCESS THEY ENJOYED IN THE AFL.

NEW ENGLAND LINEBACKER ED PHILPOTT TRIPS NEW YORK RUNNING BACK JOHN RIGGINS IN 1971. RIGGINS BEGAN HIS HALL OF FAME CAREER THAT YEAR.

The Jets had returned to the playoffs the season after they won the Super Bowl. They then entered a period in which they did not have much success. Namath and the team showed occasional flashes of brilliance. Namath's injuries forced him out of the lineup for long periods, though. He sometimes played poorly when he returned.

The Jets had a rematch with the Colts in their fifth game as NFL members. Namath suffered a broken right wrist but made it through the 29–22 loss. However, he did not play again the rest of the season. The Jets' first season as a member of the NFL ended with a 4–10 record.

Namath missed more than a year of regular-season action. After recovering from the wrist injury, he injured his left knee while trying to make a tackle on a fumble return in a 1971 preseason game. The injury required surgery. Namath would not return to the field until the eleventh game of the 1971 campaign.

The best two seasons the Jets could produce with Namath in the NFL were 1972 and 1974. Even then, the Jets went 7–7 both times.

The team's biggest offensive stars of the 1970s each had their moments in the 1972 season.

Namath got the show started on September 24 when he and the Jets beat the Colts

JOHN RIGGINS

Running back John Riggins began a Hall of Fame career with the Jets. New York selected the former University of Kansas star with a first-round draft pick, sixth overall, in 1971. He played for the Jets from 1971 to 1975.

Riggins rushed for 769 yards and caught 36 passes as a rookie. He ran for 944 yards the next season. In his final year in New York, Riggins became the first player in team history to rush for more than 1,000 yards in a season. He ran for 1,005 yards and eight touchdowns.

Nicknamed "The Diesel," Riggins finished his career with the Washington Redskins (1976–79 and 1981–85). The 6-foot-2, 230-pounder ended his career with 11,352 rushing yards and 104 touchdowns. He was named MVP of Super Bowl XVII after running for 166 yards, including a go-ahead 43-yard touchdown, in Washington's 27–17 win over Miami.

and Johnny Unitas in a 44–34 victory. The teams set what was then a league record by combining for 872 passing yards. Namath threw for 496 yards and six touchdowns.

The backfield combination of John Riggins and Emerson Boozer starred on October 15. Riggins ran for 168 yards and Boozer 150 in a 41–13 rout of the Patriots. The Jets totaled a team-record 333 rushing yards.

Don Maynard passed Raymond Berry and became professional football's all-time leader in receptions. Maynard made career catch number 632 during a 24–16 loss to the Oakland Raiders on *Monday Night Football* on December 11.

The Jets were on the wrong end of a record-setting day the next year. Weeb Ewbank's coaching career came to an end on December 16, 1973. The Bills pounded the Jets 34–14 at Shea Stadium. O. J. Simpson ran for 200 yards. That gave him 2,003 for 1973 and made him the first runner in NFL history to top 2,000 in a season.

While the .500 season in 1972 was disappointing, the same record in 1974 created reason for hope. That year, the Jets turned a 1–7 record around by winning their final six games. However, the team was not able to continue that success.

Three years after Ewbank left the sideline, Namath was gone too. Namath threw just four touchdown passes while being intercepted 16 times in 1976. He was let go after the season.

Walt Michaels took over in 1977 and coached the team through its third straight 3–11 season. The NFL expanded its

JOE NAMATH, *LEFT*, POSES WITH ROOKIE RICHARD TODD IN 1976. TODD TOOK OVER AS THE JETS' STARTING QUARTERBACK IN 1977.

schedule to 16 games the next year. The Jets made it to .500 again. They went 8–8 in both the 1978 and 1979 seasons.

The progress the team seemed to be making again lost its momentum in 1980. The Jets went just 4–12. Brighter days were ahead, though.

END OF AN ERA

Joe Namath finished his career by playing four games with the Los Angeles Rams in 1977. After Namath played for the Jets from 1965 through 1976, the team tried to honor his request for a trade to the Rams. When a trade could not be completed, the Jets released Namath. This made him free to sign with Los Angeles. Namath played in two wins and two losses with the Rams. He then retired when the season was over.

CHAPTER 4

SACK EXCHANGE

Star power shifted from the offensive to the defensive side of the ball in New York in 1981. With defensive ends Joe Klecko and Mark Gastineau leading the way, the Jets' pass rush became known as the "New York Sack Exchange." The Sack Exchange was one of the biggest reasons for the team's first winning season, 10–5–1, since the leagues merged in 1970.

Richard Todd led the passing attack. Todd had speedy wide receiver Wesley Walker, tight end Jerome Barkum, and all-purpose back Bruce Harper as his top three receivers. Todd passed for 3,231 yards and 25 touchdowns.

JOE KLECKO

The Jets' Joe Klecko made the Pro Bowl at three different positions. Klecko, a former standout at Temple University, played for the Jets from 1977 to 1987. He reached all-star status as a defensive end and a tackle in a four-man front. He was honored again after making the switch to nose tackle, the middle spot, in defensive coordinator Bud Carson's 3–4 defense.

MARK GASTINEAU WAS THE LEADER OF THE JETS' "NEW YORK SACK EXCHANGE" PASS RUSH IN THE 1980s.

THE JETS' FREEMAN MCNEIL RUNS AGAINST THE BENGALS DURING NEW YORK'S 44–17 FIRST-ROUND PLAYOFF WIN IN JANUARY 1983.

Klecko and Gastineau combined for more than 40 sacks. They were joined on the four-man defensive front by Marty Lyons and Abdul Salaam.

The Jets won seven of their final eight regular-season games. They qualified for the playoffs for the first time since 1969. However, they fell behind the visiting Buffalo Bills 24–0 in their AFC wild-card game. The Jets fought back but lost 31–27.

An NFL players' strike shortened the 1982 regular season. New York did well in the nine games that were held. Freeman McNeil became the first Jet to lead the NFL in rushing yards, gaining 786. The Jets finished the regular season 6–3. They then reached the AFC Championship Game by beating the Cincinnati Bengals 44–17 and the Los Angeles Raiders 17–14. They fell one step short of a Super Bowl, however. They lost 14–0 to the host Miami Dolphins in the AFC title game.

Coach Walt Michaels left the Jets. Offensive coordinator Joe Walton took over as coach and was unable to continue the playoff streak. New York went 7–9 in 1983. The Jets lost their final home game at Shea Stadium, 34–7 to the Pittsburgh Steelers. In 1984, they moved to Giants Stadium at the Meadowlands in northern New Jersey.

Gastineau led the league in sacks in 1983 and 1984. He set an NFL record with

MUD BOWL

The AFC Championship Game after the 1982 regular season became known as the Mud Bowl. Playing in swampy conditions at the Orange Bowl in Miami, the Jets' offense could not move.

Nearly 25 years after the 14–0 loss to Miami on January 23, 1983, coach Walt Michaels still claimed that the field did not have to be as bad as it was. He believed that Dolphins coach Don Shula wanted the field left uncovered in the rain in the days before the game to slow down the Jets' speedy offense.

"There were some things that went on," Michaels told the *New York Daily News.* "The league rule is to cover the field, and it wasn't. What else has to be said?"

The Dolphins intercepted Richard Todd five times. Linebacker A. J. Duhe had three of the interceptions. New York's Freeman McNeil rushed for just 46 yards on 17 carries in the Miami mud.

KEN O'BRIEN PASSES AGAINST THE DOLPHINS ON SEPTEMBER 21, 1986. O'BRIEN THREW FOR 479 YARDS IN THE JETS' 51–45 OVERTIME WIN.

22 sacks in 1984. However, he was unable to help the team avoid another 7–9 season. Quarterback Ken O'Brien emerged to guide a record-setting offense in 1985. O'Brien threw five touchdown passes, including three to Mickey Shuler, on November 17. The Jets had their highest-scoring game ever that day in a 62–28 win over the Tampa Bay Buccaneers. The Jets finished 11–5 and clinched another playoff trip. New York lost 26–14 to

visiting New England, though, in the AFC wild-card round.

The offense got rolling again early in the 1986 season. O'Brien and Miami's Dan Marino combined for 927 passing yards, an NFL record, when the host Jets beat the Dolphins 51–45 in overtime on September 21. Walker set a team record by catching four touchdown passes in the game. He had a 43-yard touchdown reception in overtime that won it for New York.

The shootout win over the Dolphins was the first victory in a team-record nine-game winning streak by the Jets. However, Gastineau, Klecko, linebacker Lance Mehl, and tackle Reggie McElroy all suffered knee injuries that season. The team fell apart. New York lost its final five games to finish 10–6. Gastineau returned in time for the Jets' 35–15 wild-card playoff

MARK GASTINEAU

Mark Gastineau came out of small East Central Oklahoma State University to play for the Jets from 1979 to 1988. During that time, Gastineau had plenty of opportunities to show off his celebratory dances after sacks. He led the league in sacks twice and had more than 100 in his career. Gastineau was selected as the 1984 NFL Defensive Player of the Year. He fought through injuries in 1985, 1986, and 1987. He then left the team midway through the 1988 season.

win over Kansas City. New York was eliminated in the conference semifinals, 23–20 in double overtime at Cleveland.

The Jets slipped back to losing seasons in three of the next four years. The only exception, an 8–7–1 mark in 1988, was not a cause for celebration. That was the year Klecko left the team before the season because of injuries and Gastineau retired midway through the season.

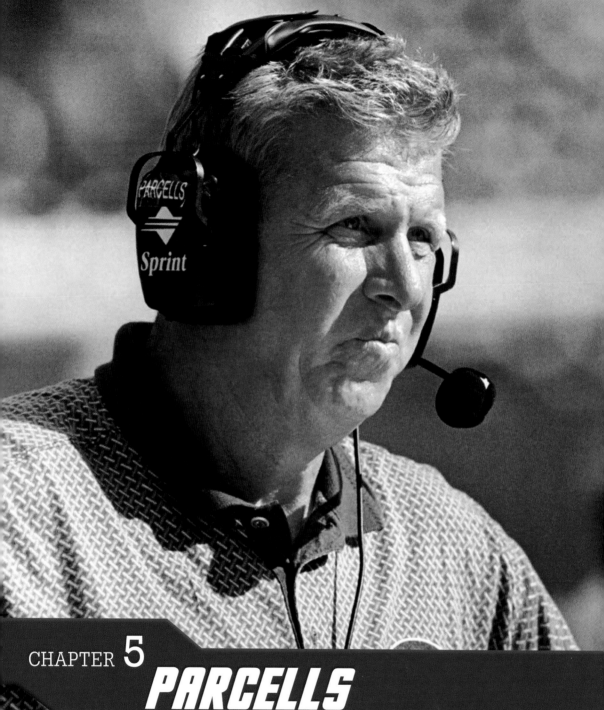

CHAPTER 5

PARCELLS IN CHARGE

The Jets struggled through the early 1990s. The team changed management, coaches, and quarterbacks. However, New York was unable to produce a winning season.

The best the team could manage from 1989 through 1996 were 8–8 marks in 1991 and 1993. In 1991, 8–8 was good enough to make the playoffs. The Jets lost 17–10 to the Houston Oilers in the first round, though.

Ken O'Brien was the starting quarterback through 1991, when he made the Pro Bowl. But O'Brien missed much of training camp in 1992 in a contract dispute. Then changes were made that eventually led to eight

INSPIRATIONAL PLAYER

Jets defensive end Dennis Byrd was partially paralyzed during a collision with teammate Scott Mersereau in the third quarter of the team's loss to Kansas City on November 29, 1992. Byrd had spinal surgery in New York on December 3. With the help of experimental treatments, he walked onto the field during a halftime ceremony on opening day in 1993. Byrd was selected for the Jets' Most Inspirational Player award. The next year, the award was named after him.

COACH BILL PARCELLS LED THE JETS TO AN AFC EAST TITLE IN 1998 AND A SPOT IN THE AFC CHAMPIONSHIP GAME.

different starting quarterbacks from 1992 through 1996.

The Jets hit rock bottom in the 1995 and 1996 seasons under coach Rich Kotite. They gave up 30 or more points in six of the final seven games under him. He went 3–13 in 1995 and 1–15 in 1996. That led to the controversial pursuit of New England coach Bill Parcells, who took over as coach and general manager.

Parcells made a big splash in his Jets debut on August 31,

1997. Neil O'Donnell threw five touchdown passes in a 41–3 romp over the Seattle Seahawks. New York produced its first winning season since 1988. However, the Jets finished 9–7 and just missed a playoff berth.

In their finest season since the Super Bowl victory, the Jets went 12–4 and won their first AFC East title in 1998. Vinny Testaverde, who signed in the offseason, took over as the starting quarterback early in the season. Testaverde threw for 3,256 yards and 29 touchdowns with just seven interceptions.

On January 10, 1999, against the Jacksonville Jaguars, wide receiver Keyshawn Johnson starred in the Jets' first playoff win since 1986. Johnson caught a touchdown pass in

NUMBER ONE PICK

In 1996, the Jets had the first overall pick in the NFL Draft for the first time. They used the pick on wide receiver Keyshawn Johnson, an All-American at the University of Southern California. Johnson caught 305 passes in four seasons with the Jets. He led them in receptions in 1997, 1998, and 1999. He grabbed passes for more than 1,000 yards in 1998 and 1999.

WIDE RECEIVER KEYSHAWN JOHNSON HAD 83 CATCHES FOR 1,131 YARDS IN 1998, WHEN THE JETS WON THE AFC EAST CHAMPIONSHIP.

TRADING FOR A COACH

Bill Parcells was unhappy but still under contract with New England when the Jets decided to make him their general manager in 1997.

The teams fought over the issue. The NFL had to get involved. During the controversy, Bill Belichick, an assistant coach on Parcells' staff with the Patriots, was going to become Jets head coach under Parcells. That plan lasted just six days, however. Belichick became assistant head coach/secondary coach for the Jets. Parcells was named head coach.

Part of the deal allowing Parcells to move to New York was the requirement that the Jets send four draft picks, including a first-rounder, to the Patriots. Belichick later won three Super Bowls—after the 2001, 2003, and 2004 seasons—as New England's head coach. The Patriots used the draft picks they acquired from the Jets to help them win those Super Bowls.

the first quarter and ran for a score in the second quarter to give the host Jets a 17–0 lead. He then preserved a 34–24 win by filling in as an extra defensive back and making a late interception. The next week, the visiting Jets led Denver 10–0 in the third quarter of the AFC Championship Game. But six turnovers contributed to a 23–10 loss to the eventual Super Bowl champion Broncos.

In the second quarter of the 1999 opener, Testaverde suffered a ruptured Achilles tendon. The injury ended his season. The team still managed an 8–8 finish. New York did not return to the playoffs, however.

QUARTERBACK VINNY TESTAVERDE PASSES AS RUNNING BACK CURTIS MARTIN BLOCKS IN NEW YORK'S 34–24 PLAYOFF WIN OVER JACKSONVILLE IN JANUARY 1999.

CHAPTER 6
FAST STARTERS

The early part of the 2000 Jets season was about comebacks. Quarterback Vinny Testaverde returned from the ruptured Achilles tendon that had ruined his 1999 season. His return led New York to a team-record 4–0 start.

That was just the beginning. On *Monday Night Football* on October 23, the Miami Dolphins opened a 30–7 third-quarter lead on the Jets. Testaverde was forced to throw 59 times to try to bring his team from behind. He made the most of those attempts. Testaverde passed for 378 yards and five touchdowns. Four of the touchdowns came during a 30-point fourth quarter that tied the score and forced overtime. John Hall's 40-yard field goal in overtime lifted the host Jets to a 40–37 victory. The game became known as the "Monday Night Miracle." The win gave New York a 6–1 start.

The Jets were about to start an unfortunate trend, however. New York had a pair of three-game losing streaks, including

JETS KICKER JOHN HALL, *LEFT*, AND HOLDER TOM TUPA CELEBRATE HALL'S 40-YARD FIELD GOAL THAT BEAT THE DOLPHINS 40–37 IN OCTOBER 2000.

HERM EDWARDS COACHED THE JETS FROM 2001 THROUGH 2005. HE GUIDED THEM TO THE PLAYOFFS IN 2001 AND 2004 WITH 10–6 RECORDS.

one to end the season, and finished 9–7. The Jets of the first decade of the twenty-first century won 15 more games than in the previous decade. They were a team that often started strong before losing steam, though.

The 2004 team began the season 5–0 but lost three of its last four to finish 10–6. A 2–3 start the next year was followed by seven straight losses and a 4–12 finish. After winning five straight games in 2008 to reach

8–3, the Jets lost four of their final five and missed the playoffs. The 2009 team won its first three games, then lost six out of seven and needed a big finish to sneak into the playoffs at 9–7.

One year, the team made its turnaround in the opposite direction. The 2006 Jets were just a .500 team before winning five of their final six to finish 10–6 and make the playoffs.

Still, the highs and lows of the 2000s produced more playoff appearances, five, than any other decade in team history. Hall's 53-yard field goal with 59 seconds left in the 2001 season finale beat the Oakland Raiders 24–22. The win also locked up the first of the five berths. The Jets had to go right back to Oakland to open the playoffs and lost the rematch 38–24.

COACH FOR A DAY

The 2000 Jets went from "coach for a day" Bill Belichick to "coach for a year" Al Groh.

Belichick, the team's assistant head coach/secondary coach, changed his mind about plans for him to replace Bill Parcells when Parcells gave up coaching duties to concentrate on his work in the front office. Groh, the linebackers coach, was promoted instead. Groh led the Jets to a 9–7 record in 2000 but decided to return to his alma mater, the University of Virginia, as head coach.

After turning down the Jets' head coaching offer, Belichick became the New England Patriots' coach. Because Belichick broke his contract in leaving, it meant that the Jets and Patriots were back to negotiating compensation for the release of a coach. This time, it was New England that sent New York a first-round pick as part of the package.

The 2002 team also made the playoffs on the final day of the regular season with a 42–17 romp over the Green Bay Packers. After blanking the Indianapolis Colts 41–0 for the first playoff shutout in team history, New York could not score in the second half at Oakland and took a 30–10 loss.

The 2004 team finished its run with three straight overtime games. New York lost to the St. Louis Rams 32–29 in overtime to end a 10–6 season. The Jets then defeated the San Diego Chargers 20–17 in overtime in the wild-card round before falling to the Pittsburgh Steelers 20–17 in the divisional round, also in overtime.

The 2006 team's big finish to the regular season included a 23–3 New Year's Eve triumph over Oakland to clinch a playoff berth. The New England Patriots were too much for the Jets while running away for a 37–16 win in the wild-card round the next week.

Brett Favre spent one year as a member of the Jets in 2008. Green Bay's former Super Bowl-winning quarterback had changed his mind about retirement and was traded away by his longtime team. His arrival in New York brought excitement to the team's fans. However, the season ended in disappointment. Favre matched Joe Namath's team record of six touchdown passes in a game in a 56–35 rout of the Arizona Cardinals on September 28. The Jets also

DID YOU KNOW?

Herm Edwards was the first coach in team history to lead the squad to the playoffs in his first season. Edwards guided the Jets to a 9–7 record in 2001. Eric Mangini in 2006 and Rex Ryan in 2009 also would lead the team to the playoffs in their first seasons as coach.

QUARTERBACK BRETT FAVRE PLAYED ONE SEASON WITH THE JETS, IN 2008, AND MADE A BIG SPLASH. THE TEAM STUMBLED LATE IN THE YEAR, THOUGH, AND DID NOT REACH THE PLAYOFFS.

ripped the Tennessee Titans 34–13, ruining the NFL's last perfect record that season at 10–0. But Favre was a big part of the team's collapse down the stretch. He tried to play through arm problems and was ineffective as the Jets did not make the playoffs.

Favre moved on after just one season. He was replaced by a rookie, Mark Sanchez. Sanchez was a first-round draft pick from the University of Southern California. Sanchez started strong, slipped, and then picked up support from the NFL's top-ranked running game and overall defense. First-year coach

Rex Ryan mistakenly said the team's playoff hopes were over after a loss dropped the Jets to 7–7.

A late surge put the team in the playoffs. Sanchez was very efficient in the wild-card round. He completed 12 of 15 passes for 185 yards in a 24–14 win over the host Cincinnati Bengals. After another upset victory, 17–14 in San Diego over the Chargers, the Jets took a halftime lead in the AFC Championship Game in Indianapolis. Quarterback Peyton Manning led the Colts back to a 30–17 win, however.

For the third time since Joe Namath starred in the most famous upset in pro football history, the Jets fell one game short of returning to the Super Bowl. With another charismatic quarterback leading the way in Sanchez, though, the future appeared to be bright.

COMEBACK AGAIN

In 2002, Chad Pennington became the second Jets quarterback to lead the NFL in passing efficiency. Tears to his rotator cuff in the 2004 and 2005 seasons appeared to damage Pennington's career. But he bounced back to win the NFL Comeback Player of the Year award—twice. He is the only player to win the award twice. Pennington was first honored in 2006 for coming back from the surgeries to lead the Jets to the playoffs. The second award came after the Jets released him to make room for Brett Favre in 2008. Pennington went to Miami, where he led the Dolphins' improvement from 1–15 to 11–5.

JETS ROOKIE QUARTERBACK MARK SANCHEZ GIVES A SIGNAL AGAINST THE CHARGERS IN A PLAYOFF GAME IN JANUARY 2010. NEW YORK WON 17–14.

TIMELINE

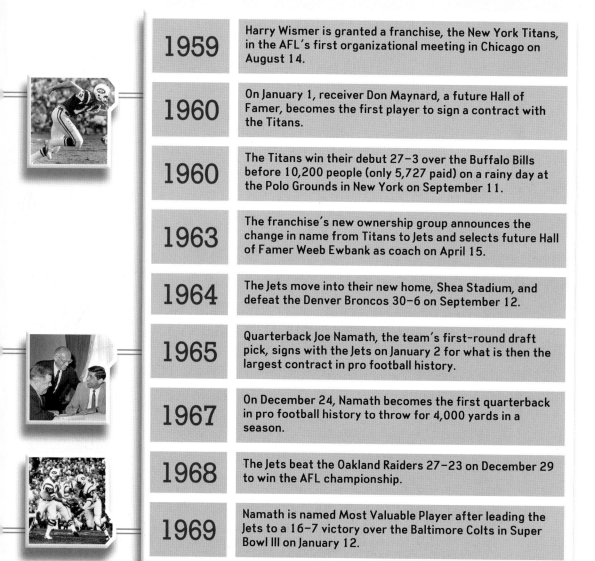

1959 — Harry Wismer is granted a franchise, the New York Titans, in the AFL's first organizational meeting in Chicago on August 14.

1960 — On January 1, receiver Don Maynard, a future Hall of Famer, becomes the first player to sign a contract with the Titans.

1960 — The Titans win their debut 27–3 over the Buffalo Bills before 10,200 people (only 5,727 paid) on a rainy day at the Polo Grounds in New York on September 11.

1963 — The franchise's new ownership group announces the change in name from Titans to Jets and selects future Hall of Famer Weeb Ewbank as coach on April 15.

1964 — The Jets move into their new home, Shea Stadium, and defeat the Denver Broncos 30–6 on September 12.

1965 — Quarterback Joe Namath, the team's first-round draft pick, signs with the Jets on January 2 for what is then the largest contract in pro football history.

1967 — On December 24, Namath becomes the first quarterback in pro football history to throw for 4,000 yards in a season.

1968 — The Jets beat the Oakland Raiders 27–23 on December 29 to win the AFL championship.

1969 — Namath is named Most Valuable Player after leading the Jets to a 16–7 victory over the Baltimore Colts in Super Bowl III on January 12.

1970 The Jets play their first game as a member of the NFL and in the first *Monday Night Football* game in a 31–21 loss to the Cleveland Browns on September 21.

1972 Namath completes 15 of 28 passes for 496 yards and six touchdowns in a 44–34 win over the Colts on September 24.

1981 The Jets lose in their first NFL playoff appearance, 31–27 to the Buffalo Bills, on December 27.

1983 The Miami Dolphins beat the visiting Jets 14–0 in an AFC Championship Game on January 23 that became known as the Mud Bowl because of the poor field conditions.

1985 On August 3, Namath becomes the first Jets player to be enshrined in the Pro Football Hall of Fame.

1986 Ken O'Brien throws for 479 yards and Miami's Dan Marino passes for 448 as the Jets beat the Dolphins 51–45 in overtime on September 21.

1997 Bill Parcells is named head coach of the Jets on February 11.

2000 The Jets score 30 fourth-quarter points and then beat the Dolphins 40–37 in overtime in the "Monday Night Miracle" on October 23.

2008 Brett Favre throws six touchdown passes in a 56–35 victory over the Arizona Cardinals on September 28.

2010 The Indianapolis Colts rally for 17 unanswered points in the second half of a 30–17 victory over the Jets in the AFC Championship Game on January 24.

QUICK STATS

FRANCHISE HISTORY
New York Titans (1960–62)
New York Jets (1963–)

SUPER BOWLS
(wins in bold)
1968 (III)

AFL CHAMPIONSHIP GAMES
(1960–69; wins in bold)
1968

AFC CHAMPIONSHIP GAMES
(since 1970 AFL-NFL merger)
1982, 1998, 2009

DIVISION CHAMPIONSHIPS
(since 1970 AFL-NFL merger)
1998, 2002

KEY PLAYERS
(position, seasons with team)
Wayne Chrebet (WR, 1995–2005)
Mark Gastineau (DE, 1979–88)
Joe Klecko (DT/DE, 1977–87)
Pat Leahy (K, 1974–91)
Curtis Martin (RB, 1998–2005)
Kevin Mawae (C, 1998–2005)
Don Maynard (WR, 1960–72)
Freeman McNeil (RB, 1981–92)
Joe Namath (QB, 1965–76)
Ken O'Brien (QB, 1984–92)
Matt Snell (FB, 1964–72)
Al Toon (WR, 1985–92)

KEY COACHES
Weeb Ewbank (1963–73):
    71–77–6; 2–1 (playoffs)
Bill Parcells (1997–99):
    29–19–0; 1–1 (playoffs)

HOME FIELDS
New Meadowlands Stadium (2010–)
Giants Stadium (1984–2009)
Shea Stadium (1964–83)
Polo Grounds (1960–63)

* All statistics through 2009 season

QUOTES AND ANECDOTES

New York Jets quarterback Richard Todd and fullback Clark Gaines put up record-setting numbers in a losing effort on September 21, 1980. Todd set an NFL record for completions in a game. The mark has since been broken. He had 42 completions in 60 attempts for 447 yards and three touchdowns in a 37–27 loss to the San Francisco 49ers. Gaines caught 17 passes. That remained the team record through 2009.

The Jets were not always comfortable at Shea Stadium, their home field for two decades. A team statement, announcing the move to Giants Stadium in East Rutherford, New Jersey, in 1984, summed up those feelings. In the release, the Jets described Shea Stadium as "rundown, neglected and the NFL's poorest facility for athletes and spectators alike."

The kelly green in the Jets' uniform colors is the same as the color used at Hess gas stations. Leon Hess owned at least part of the team from 1963 until his death in 1999.

On April 15, 2000, the Jets became the first team to make four first-round selections in the NFL Draft. They took defensive end Shaun Ellis twelfth, defensive end John Abraham thirteenth, quarterback Chad Pennington eighteenth, and tight end Anthony Becht twenty-seventh.

David A. "Sonny" Werblin, who headed the group that bought the bankrupt team in 1963, later went on to build the Meadowlands Sports Complex and manage Madison Square Garden.

GLOSSARY

American Football League

A professional football league that operated from 1960 to 1969 before merging with the National Football League.

bankrupt

Financially ruined; a company or person who has less money and assets than money owed.

berth

A place, spot, or position, such as in the NFL playoffs.

comeback

Coming from behind to take a lead in a particular game.

contract

A binding agreement about, for example, years of commitment by a football player in exchange for a given salary.

draft

A system used by professional sports leagues to select new players in order to spread incoming talent among all teams.

guarantee

A promise or assurance that something will happen.

inspirational

Stirring, motivating, or encouraging.

merge

To unite into a single body.

retire

To officially end one's career.

rookie

A first-year professional athlete.

rupture

The act of breaking or bursting.

wild card

Playoff berths given to the best remaining teams that did not win their respective divisions.

FOR MORE INFORMATION

FURTHER READING

Gruver, Ed. *From Baltimore to Broadway: Joe, the Jets, and the Super Bowl III Guarantee.* Chicago: Triumph Books, 2009.

New York Times. *New York Times Greatest Moments in New York Jets History.* New York: New York Times Publishing, 2009.

Serby, Steve. *No Substitute for Sundays: Brett Favre and His Year in the Huddle with the New York Jets.* Hoboken, NJ: John Wiley & Sons, 2009.

WEB LINKS

To learn more about the New York Jets, visit ABDO Publishing Company online at **www.abdopublishing.com**. Web sites about the Jets are featured on our Book Links page. These links are routinely monitored and updated to provide the most current information available.

PLACES TO VISIT

New Meadowlands Stadium
50 State Highway 120
East Rutherford, NJ 07073
201-935-3900
www.newmeadowlandsstadium.com
This 82,000-seat stadium is the new home of the Jets starting in the 2010 season.

Pro Football Hall of Fame
2121 George Halas Drive Northwest
Canton, OH 44708
330-456-8207
www.profootballhof.com
This hall of fame and museum highlights the greatest players and moments in the history of the National Football League. Six people affiliated with the Jets—including quarterback Joe Namath, wide receiver Don Maynard, and coach Weeb Ewbank—were enshrined as of 2010.

SUNY Cortland
P.O. Box 2000
Cortland, NY 13045
607-753-2011
The upstate New York college campus became the home of Jets training camp in the summer of 2009. Visitors to training camp can enjoy interactive activities and seek player autographs.

INDEX

About the Author

Tom Robinson is a sportswriter and an author and editor of educational books. The Clarks Summit, Pennsylvania, resident has covered National Football League games and issues during three decades of writing about sports. He has written more than 20 books for young readers.